UP A TREE

Green Tree Pythons

Willow Clark

PowerKiDS
press.

New York

Published in 2012 by The Rosen Publishing Group, Inc.
29 East 21st Street, New York, NY 10010

First Edition

Editor: Joanne Randolph
Book Design: Greg Tucker
Layout Design: Ashley Drago

Photo Credits: Cover, pp. 9, 10 (left, right), 14 (left, right), 17, 18, 19, 22 Shutterstock.com; p. 4 Stephen Cooper/Getty Images; p. 5 © www.iStockphoto.com/Kevdog818; p. 6 © www.iStockphoto.com/Shannon Plummer; p. 8 (left) © age fotostock/SuperStock; p. 8 (bottom) iStockphoto/Thinkstock; p. 11 Joe McDonald/Getty Images; pp. 12–13 © Lonely Planet/SuperStock; p. 15 © Jean-Louis Klein & Marie-Luce Hubert/Peter Arnold, Inc.; p. 16 © www.iStockphoto.com/ Mark Kostich; p. 20 © www.iStockphoto.com/Paul Tessier; p. 21 Carol Farneti Foster/Getty Images.

Library of Congress Cataloging-in-Publication Data

Clark, Willow.
 Green tree pythons / by Willow Clark. — 1st ed.
    p. cm. — (Up a tree)
 Includes index.
 ISBN 978-1-4488-6187-3 (library binding) — ISBN 978-1-4488-6333-4 (pbk.) —
ISBN 978-1-4488-6334-1 (6-pack)
 1. Green tree python—Juvenile literature. I. Title.
 QL666.O67C53 2012
 597.96'78—dc23
                          2011030141

Manufactured in the United States of America

CPSIA Compliance Information: Batch #WW12PK: For Further Information contact Rosen Publishing, New York, New York at 1-800-237-9932

Contents

Meet the Green Tree Python   4

Life in the Rain Forest   6

The Green Tree Python's Body   8

Wrap It Up   10

It's a Fact!   12

It's the Pits!   14

Python Prey   16

Python Predators   18

Hatchlings   20

Danger!   22

Glossary   23

Index   24

Web Sites   24

Meet the Green Tree Python

Did you know that some snakes climb trees? The green tree python is one of them. This **arboreal** reptile spends most of its time in trees. It spends more time in the treetops than any of the world's tree snakes.

Like other pythons, the green tree python is not a poisonous snake. Instead, it is a **constrictor**. That means it

Green tree pythons have strong muscles that let them grip tree trunks and branches tightly as they climb.

4

Green tree pythons spend the day resting in trees. At night they wait in the branches until an animal comes near. Then it is dinnertime!

uses the strong muscles in its body to squeeze its **prey** until it stops breathing and dies. This book will teach you more about the life of this snake.

Life in the Rain Forest

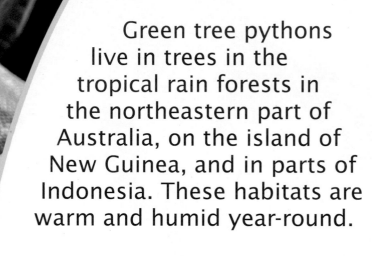

Green tree pythons live in trees in the tropical rain forests in the northeastern part of Australia, on the island of New Guinea, and in parts of Indonesia. These habitats are warm and humid year-round.

Green tree pythons like to live in the rain forest **canopy**, or the upper parts of the forest. Where green tree pythons like to live within this habitat changes throughout their lives,

This green tree python is at the top of a frangipani tree, which is a common tree in the rain forests of Southeast Asia.

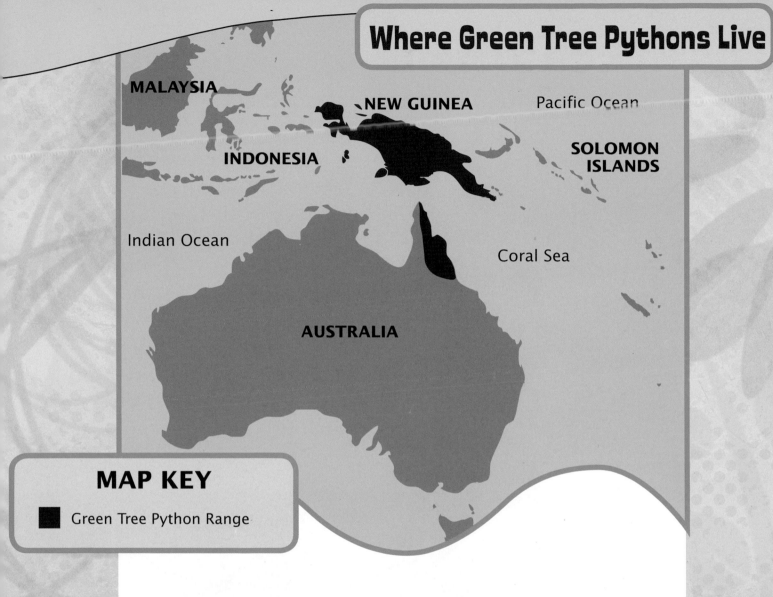

Where Green Tree Pythons Live

MALAYSIA

NEW GUINEA

Pacific Ocean

INDONESIA

SOLOMON ISLANDS

Indian Ocean

Coral Sea

AUSTRALIA

MAP KEY

■ Green Tree Python Range

though. When they are young, these snakes tend to live where the canopy is thinner. As adults, they move to parts of the rain forest where the canopy is thicker.

The Green Tree Python's Body

There is only one **species** of green tree python. These snakes can have lots of different colors and patterns, though. They have yellowish bellies and are green along their backs. The shades of green found on these snakes range from bluish to bright emerald green. Some have blue or white spots on their backs or sides, too.

Above: This may not look like a green tree python, but it is! Young snakes can be red, orange, or yellow. Some adults have different colors, too. *Right*: Green tree pythons have heads shaped a bit like triangles. Their mouths can open really wide to let them swallow animals without chewing them.

A full-grown green tree python is about 5 feet (1.5 m) long. Its body is muscular, with a short, diamond-shaped head. Like many arboreal animals, green tree pythons have **prehensile** tails, which helps them grip tree branches.

Some green tree pythons can look almost blue. Can you see the yellow belly on this one?

Wrap It Up

Green tree pythons have a special way of wrapping their bodies around tree branches when they are resting. They coil their bodies around horizontal branches and rest their heads on the middle of their bodies. This gives them a way to rest while staying balanced on tree branches. When the snake is ready to hunt, it wraps its tail around a branch

Some people think green tree pythons rest in their special way to trick predators. The predators think they are looking at bunches of bananas!

This green tree python is ready to hunt prey.

but keeps its head or the front part of its body uncoiled. This leaves it ready to attack its prey. Green tree pythons generally change from a resting to a hunting position at either dawn or dusk. This helps them keep from being seen by any interested **predators**.

It's a Fact!

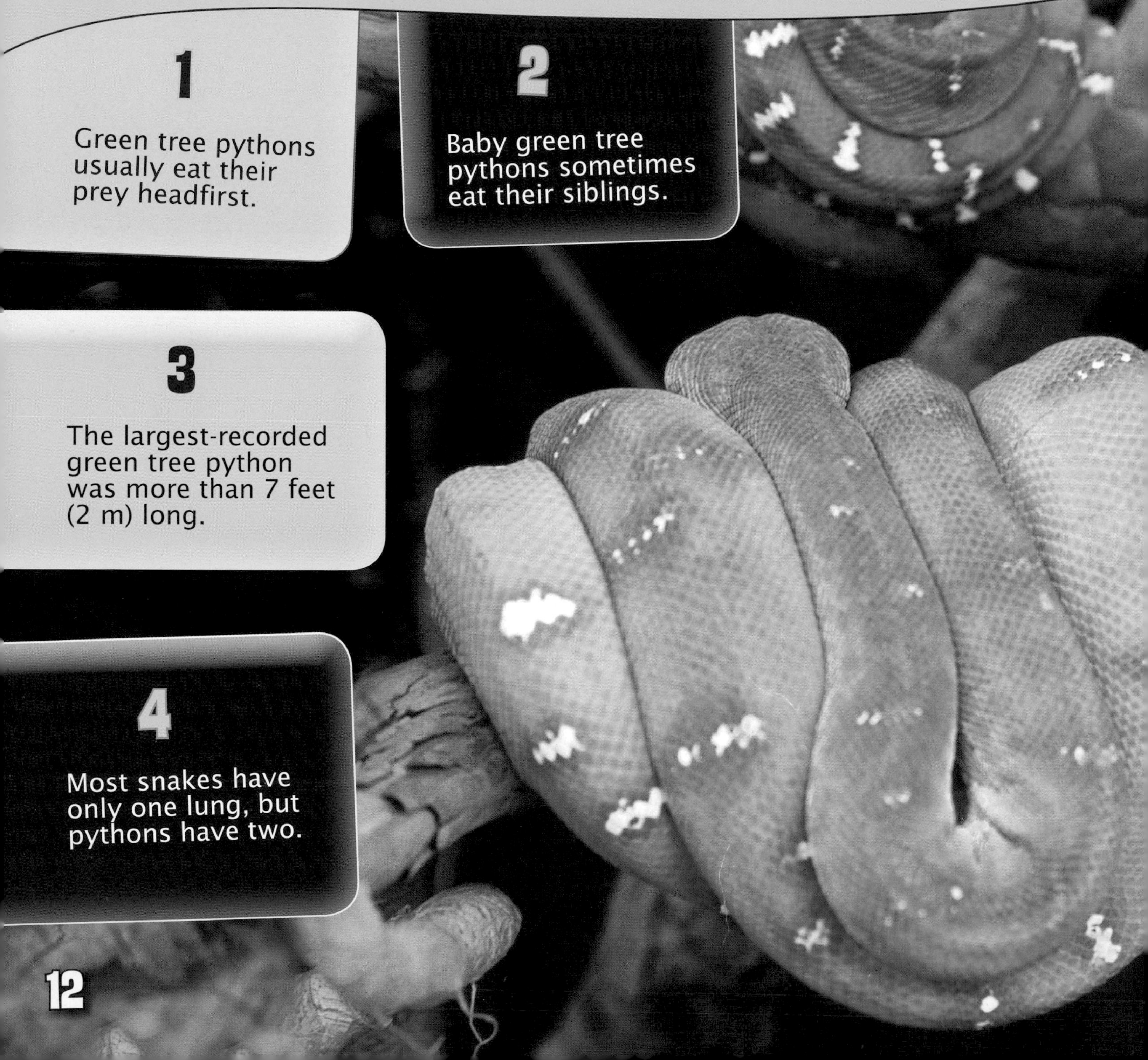

1

Green tree pythons usually eat their prey headfirst.

2

Baby green tree pythons sometimes eat their siblings.

3

The largest-recorded green tree python was more than 7 feet (2 m) long.

4

Most snakes have only one lung, but pythons have two.

5

Green tree pythons sometimes wiggle the tips of their tails to attract prey.

6

Even though they are **cold-blooded**, female green tree pythons can "shiver" around their eggs to keep the eggs warm.

7

A group of snake eggs is called a clutch.

8

The oldest-recorded green tree python lived to be 20 years old.

9

In Papua New Guinea, the green tree python is hunted for food.

It's the Pits!

Green tree pythons use their eyes and noses to hunt. They also have heat-sensing pits that help them find prey. These pits are near their upper lips. With the help of the pits, they can sense prey in the dark or among a thick cover of leaves.

Scientists believe that these pits do more than help green

Above: The green tree python's pits are between their lips and eyes. They can pick up even tiny changes in temperature. This makes it hard for rats and mice to hide from them. *Right*: Green tree pythons, like all snakes, do not have eyelids. Their eyes cannot move much. They count on their senses of smell and touch to hunt, not their eyesight.

Snakes do not use their noses to smell. They use their tongues! The tongue carries small bits of odor to a special organ on the roof of the snake's mouth.

tree pythons when they are hunting. Just as the pits help them find prey, they also help the pythons stay away from predators that want to eat them. Scientists also think that because these snakes are cold-blooded, as are all reptiles, the pits help them find places to warm up.

Python Prey

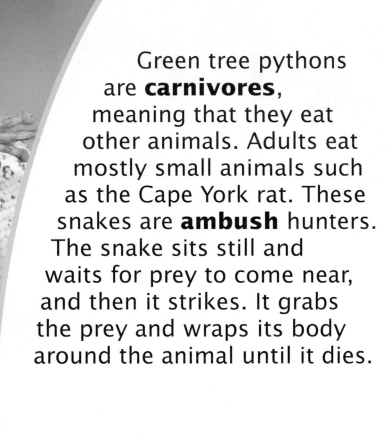

Green tree pythons are **carnivores**, meaning that they eat other animals. Adults eat mostly small animals such as the Cape York rat. These snakes are **ambush** hunters. The snake sits still and waits for prey to come near, and then it strikes. It grabs the prey and wraps its body around the animal until it dies.

The green tree python eats rodents, frogs, and other small animals. It squeezes the prey so hard that it cannot breathe and it dies.

A green tree python would be happy to make a meal out of a large rodent like this one.

After the prey is caught and killed, the green tree python **unhinges** its jaw. By doing this, it is able to swallow the prey whole. The snake's strong muscles pull the prey down its throat and into its stomach.

Python Predators

Although the green tree python is a predator, it is also prey to other animals. Birds such as raptors, goshawks, and eagles eat green tree pythons. Reptiles such as mangrove monitors hunt the green tree python, too.

Many birds, such as the kookaburra, will eat young snakes. It would take a larger raptor to be able to eat a full-grown tree python, though!

The main way that green tree pythons avoid predators is by **camouflage**, or blending in with their surroundings. Their green

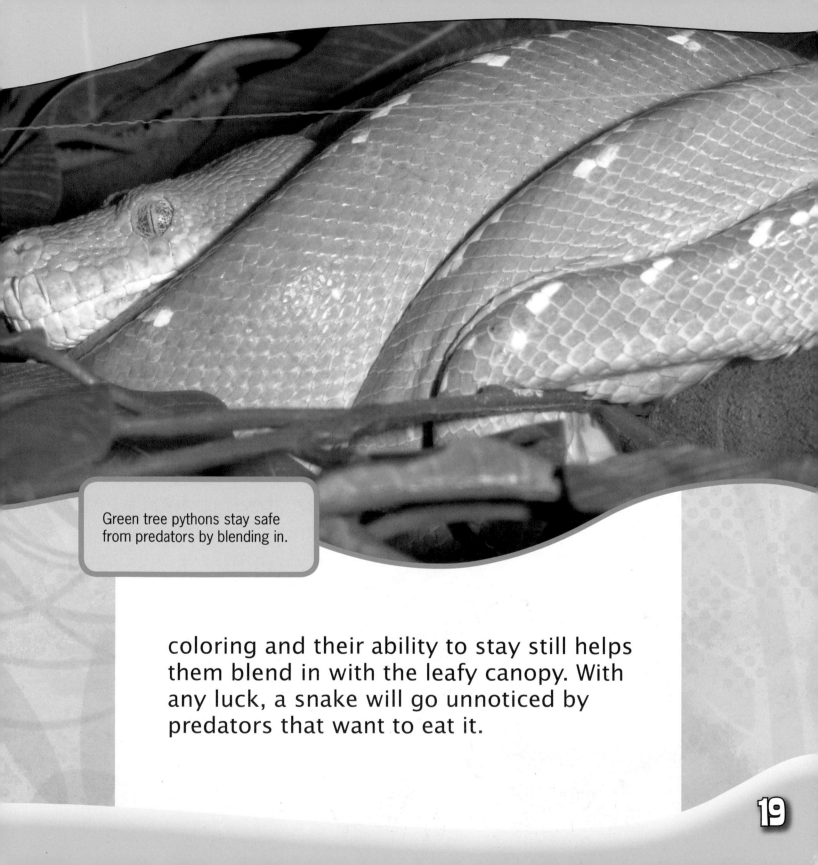

Green tree pythons stay safe from predators by blending in.

coloring and their ability to stay still helps them blend in with the leafy canopy. With any luck, a snake will go unnoticed by predators that want to eat it.

Hatchlings

Green tree pythons are solitary animals. This means that they live alone and come together only to **mate**. After mating, the female lays her eggs in a tree hollow. She may lay between 6 and 30 eggs. Most python mothers coil themselves around their eggs during the six to eight weeks it takes for them to **hatch**. After the babies come out of their eggs, the mother leaves them.

This green tree python is hatching from its egg. The egg casing is soft and leathery, not hard like a chicken's egg.

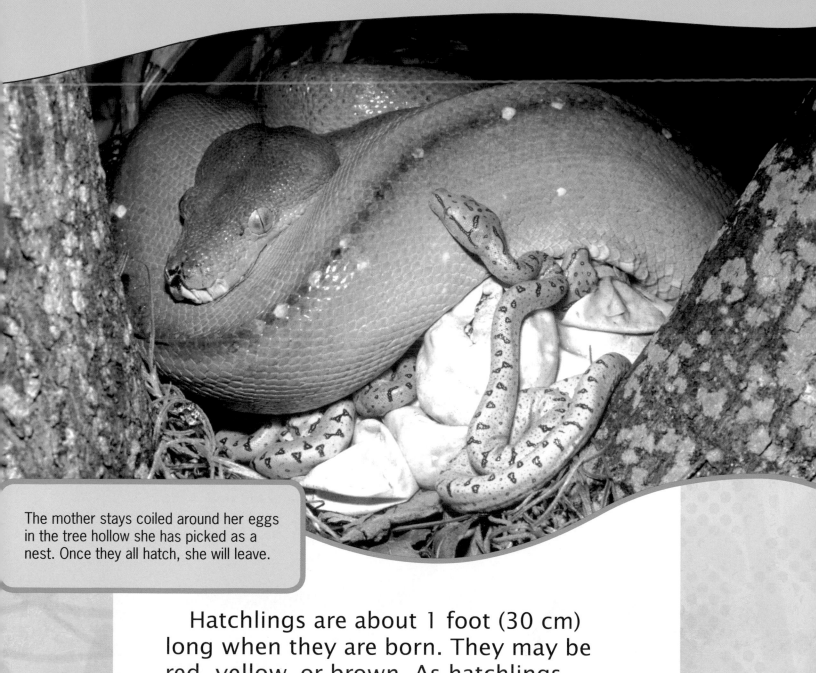

The mother stays coiled around her eggs in the tree hollow she has picked as a nest. Once they all hatch, she will leave.

Hatchlings are about 1 foot (30 cm) long when they are born. They may be red, yellow, or brown. As hatchlings grow, their color changes to bright green. They reach adulthood at about age three.

Danger!

The green tree python is not an **endangered** species, but that does not mean that it does not face any dangers. Many people want to keep green tree pythons as pets. Many of these snakes are taken from the wild illegally. If people take too many snakes from the wild, it upsets the balance in nature.

Green tree pythons are also at risk when their rain forest habitat is cut down for logging or to build farms. Today people are working to make laws to save parts of these rain forests. This helps all of the plants and animals in the habitat, including the green tree python.

Green tree pythons deserve our respect, as do all animals. We need to leave them in their natural habitat and keep that habitat safe.

Glossary

ambush (AM-bush) To attack by surprise from a hiding place.

arboreal (ahr-BOR-ee-ul) Having to do with trees.

camouflage (KA-muh-flahj) A color or shape that matches what is around something and helps hide it.

canopy (KA-nuh-pee) The highest tree canopes in a forest.

carnivores (KAHR-neh-vorz) Animals that eat only other animals.

cold-blooded (KOHLD-bluh-did) Having body heat that changes with the heat around the body.

constrictor (kun-STRIKT-ur) A snake that kills by wrapping its body around its prey and squeezing.

endangered (in-DAYN-jerd) In danger of no longer living.

hatch (HACH) To come out of an egg.

mate (MAYT) To come together to make babies.

predators (PREH-duh-terz) Animals that kill other animals for food.

prehensile (pree-HEN-sul) Can catch by going around.

prey (PRAY) An animal that is hunted by another animal for food.

species (SPEE-sheez) One kind of living thing. All people are one species.

unhinges (un-HINJ-ez) Takes off of a joint.

Index

A
Australia, 6

B
branch(es), 9–10

C
canopy, 6–7, 19
clutch, 13

E
eggs, 13, 20
eyes, 14

F
farms, 22
food, 13

H
habitat(s), 6, 22
head(s), 9–11

I
Indonesia, 6

J
jaw, 17

L
lips, 14
lung, 12

M
mangrove monitors, 18
muscles, 5, 17

N
noses, 14

P
Papua New Guinea, 13
patterns, 8
pets, 22

pits, 14–15
predator(s), 11, 15, 18–19
prey, 5, 11–18

R
rain forest(s), 6–7, 22
raptors, 18
reptile(s), 4, 15, 18

S
scientists, 14–15
siblings, 12
snake(s), 4, 5, 7, 8, 10, 12, 15–16, 19, 22
species, 8, 22
spots, 8
stomach, 17

T
trees, 4, 6

Web Sites

Due to the changing nature of Internet links, PowerKids Press has developed an online list of Web sites related to the subject of this book. This site is updated regularly. Please use this link to access the list:
www.powerkidslinks.com/uptr/python/